Original title:
Burritos and Blankets

Copyright © 2024 Creative Arts Management OÜ
All rights reserved.

Author: Colin Harrington
ISBN HARDBACK: 978-9916-94-278-9
ISBN PAPERBACK: 978-9916-94-279-6

Wrapped Dreams

In a tortilla snug as a bug,
Rolling flavors in a cozy hug.
With beans and cheese all piled high,
Like a dream in the night sky.

A dash of spice, a twirl of zest,
Each bite a jest, it's simply the best.
Salsa sizzles, what a delight,
Giggles erupt with every bite.

Cozy Creations

Layers wrapped in a savory pact,
Mismatched delights, what a tasty act!
Guacamole splatters, a green surprise,
You just can't be serious with such tasty pies!

Sitting warm in a colorful fold,
These delicious treasures, stories untold.
Tortilla smiles, what a sight to see,
Each crunch and munch, a wild jubilee!

The Warm Embrace of Flavor

A fiesta rolls in, spices amass,
Wrapped in joy, they dance with class.
Each bite a giggle, a hearty cheer,
Flavor explosions, oh my dear!

Syrupy sauces dribble down,
Dancing with laughter, all wearing crowns.
Mexican magic, all piled high,
With every chomp, we soar in the sky.

Tucked in Comfort

In folds so soft, like a hug from mom,
Each delicate layer begins to charm.
Avocado whispers, spicy and bold,
A cozy cocoon, a story unfold.

Each munch a cuddle, a playful tease,
With laughter that floats like a warm breeze.
Wrapped snug and tight, it's joy on a plate,
Who knew comfort could be this great!

Bite-sized Hugs

Wrapped up tight, a cozy treat,
A tortilla hug, oh so neat.
With beans and cheese, they dance around,
After one bite, joy is found.

Spicy salsa, a zesty glance,
In every roll, a tasty chance.
Each little morsel, a joyful sigh,
Who needs the sun when food's this high?

Flavorful Fractions

Take one portion, just a slice,
Add some guac, oh how nice!
A pinch of zest, a dash of flair,
It's a fiesta, beware the chair!

With every layer, laughter grows,
Sour cream smiles and funny pose.
You'll find joy in every bite,
As flavors mingle, pure delight!

Enfolded Delicacies

Beneath the wrap, magic awaits,
A treasure chest of tasty fates.
Chili whispers, corn can twirl,
In each little roll, life's a whirl!

Folded soft like a cozy bed,
With every taste, a chuckle spread.
Friends gather 'round, a feast so grand,
With saucy tales, we make our stand!

Gourmet Nest

In a warm cocoon, flavors blend,
Each crunchy bite, a joyful trend.
Wrap them well, like a hug so tight,
In this gourmet nest, we dine with delight.

Mouth-watering nibbles, a savory scene,
Sauces drip down, a foodie dream.
Laughter erupts, as we devour,
This cozy meal; it's our power hour!

Spice and Snuggle

Wrapped up tight in flavors bold,
Warmth surrounds, we shiver not cold.
A twist of zest, a pinch of cheer,
Laughter erupts when friends are near.

Crispy edges, a cheesy grin,
In cozy wraps, the fun begins.
Each bite a hug, so snug and bright,
In our feast, the world feels right.

Tucked in Tastes

Rolled up joy with a dash of glee,
Salsa dances, a sight to see.
Crispy crunch, then creamy bliss,
In every wrap, a flavor kiss.

A snuggle here, a bite or two,
Spices mingle, a party for two.
When the night is chilly and long,
With tasty wraps, we can't go wrong.

Comfort in a Fold

Tucked in warmth that never ends,
Waves of flavor, like sunlit bends.
A pinch of humor, a splash of zest,
In cozy layers, we feel so blessed.

Friends unite, with smiles that beam,
A crunchy shell, the ultimate dream.
In each plush layer, we find delight,
Contentment rolls in every bite.

Culinary Embrace

Snugly rolled, each flavor's tight,
Harmony in every single bite.
Sour and sweet combine so fine,
Together we taste, and all is divine.

In laughter's arms, we laugh our fill,
The warmth of tasty wraps, what a thrill!
A friendly wrap, a cozy chat,
With every taste, we tip our hat.

Tasty Comfort

Wrapped up tight, oh what a sight,
A feast in hand, that feels just right.
Spicy delight, with beans so bold,
A cozy hug, life's savory mold.

Each bite's a giggle, a crunchy cheer,
Softness surrounds, nothing to fear.
Toppings galore, a comical blend,
In this joyful dance, we gladly spend.

Snug Encounters

Late night snacks in a comfy nook,
Warming our hearts like a cozy book.
Salsa drips, laughter fills the air,
In our happy spot, we haven't a care.

Twists and turns, a spicy embrace,
In a tasty world, we find our place.
Ultimate fluff, a funny flair,
Nestled together, we're quite the pair.

Flavor in a Furl

Roll it up tight, what a grand tease,
Every layer's a giggle, a flavor breeze.
Wraps like a hug, and oh so neat,
A delightful mix, what a crunchy treat.

The cumin dances, while cheese takes a spin,
In this zany feast, we laugh and we grin.
Unraveling joy, with every small bite,
Together we munch, the world feels just right.

Layered Lovelies

A tower of colors, a mound of cheer,
Each morsel bites, bringing us near.
Sour cream swirls, like clouds of delight,
Bursting with joys, a hilarious sight.

Each wrap a tale, with humor to share,
Gobbling them down, without a care.
In the folds we find laughter, oh what a thrill,
Layered and lovely, they fit just to fill.

Softness Served

In a wrap so snug, and oh so tight,
I find my joy, a pure delight.
Creamy beans play hide and seek,
While salsa dances, cheek to cheek.

A sprinkle of cheese, a dash of flair,
Each bite's a hug, beyond compare.
A fiesta rolls right on my plate,
With laughter and spice, it's never late.

Edible Envelopes

Packages of joy with fillings to taste,
In warm embrace, there's never waste.
Guacamole dreams in soft, warm wraps,
Each bite brings giggles, and savory snaps.

A treasure chest of flavors abound,
With every nibble, happiness found.
Rolled snugly tight, a flavorful spree,
Wrapped in laughter, come share with me.

Toasty Treats

Crispy edges, warmth divine,
These savory hugs, oh how they shine!
With crunchy bits, and spice galore,
Each bite is fun, can't help but roar.

Gather 'round for a hearty feast,
Smiles and chuckles, they never cease.
In nutty wraps, and cheesy folds,
The magic lies in tales retold.

Hugging Hues

Colorful layers stacked up high,
With each unfolding, my spirits fly.
Pico de gallo, a zesty swirl,
Each bite a giggle, a flavor whirl.

Soft and cozy, my joy is near,
Wrapped in warmth, I shed all fear.
In every bundle, a chuckle awaits,
A feast of colors on my plates.

Sauced in Softness

Rolled up tightly, oh so bold,
A wrap of dreams, of flavors told.
Salsa drips like laughter's song,
In every bite, where we belong.

Soft embrace, a cozy feast,
With every crunch, we love the least.
Under the sauce, we giggle and cheer,
This joyful wrap brings us near!

Nighttime munchies, snuggled right,
Dancing flavors, pure delight.
The pillow food uncurls our grins,
As flavor wins, the laughter spins.

Culinary Cuddles

Gather 'round for a tasty hug,
Wrapped in warmth, a cozy drug.
Beans and cheese, a tender kiss,
Spices whirl, we shan't miss.

A rolling party, what a scene,
Forget your troubles, join the cuisine.
Every bite's a chuckle sound,
In this soft wrap, joy is found.

Chewy and warm, a delightful muse,
Filling our hearts while we amuse.
Laughter flows like melted cheese,
In this creation, we find our ease.

Whispers of Spice and Softness

Gentle whispers wrapped in love,
Spices dance, it's what we're dreaming of.
In a cozy shell, we take a ride,
Two flavors merge, side by side.

Crunchy bites with a hint of fun,
A tasty tale for everyone.
Wrapped in warmth, we softly share,
Laughter twinkles in the air.

Saucy secrets, with smiles they weave,
Joking around, it's hard to believe.
With every fill, we hum a tune,
As joy unfolds beneath the moon.

Enveloped in Bliss

Cuddled morsels, oh what a sight,
In layers of joy, we unite.
Flavors twirl in a dance so grand,
A feast of laughter, hand in hand.

Each tender bite is a playful tease,
Wrapped in fun, we say, "More, please!"
Happiness drips from the edges wide,
In this fluffy nest, we take pride.

Comfort unfolds with every chew,
It's a giggly ride, just me and you.
From crunch to soft in a wink,
This tasty joy makes us all think.

Plush Pleasures

In a wrap so snug, a tasty feast,
Cheese and beans dance, a flavor beast.
Folded tightly, a hearty hug,
Every bite, my soul is dug.

Salsa splatters, oh what a scene,
Laughing hard, it's so obscene.
Guacamole slips, it's quite a fight,
A delicious struggle, my appetite's delight.

Warmth-on-a-Plate

A sizzling treat, my plate's a thrill,
Spices ignite with an eager chill.
Wrapped so cozy, a savory race,
Each mouthful's a hug, a warm embrace.

Dripping goodness, sauce on my chin,
How did I get this joy in my skin?
Ever so comfy, I'm sinking deep,
In layers of flavors, my taste buds leap.

Gastronomic Cocoon

Inside this wrap, I'm safely tied,
Like a snug bug, I can't hide.
Lettuce whispers, the rice does sing,
Together they bring a tasty fling.

A cuddly mound, rolled just right,
Filling me up, oh what a sight!
With every crunch, laughter flows,
In this cocoon, my spirit grows.

Edible Cuddle

With each bite, I feel so spry,
A soft embrace that makes me sigh.
Layers of joy, so stacked with care,
Every morsel feels like a dare.

Wrapped in warmth, I take a chance,
As flavors swirl, I find my dance.
Giggles erupt with every taste,
In this edible hug, I feel no haste.

Emollient Edibles

In a wrap of warmth I hide,
With cheesy dreams and beans inside.
Rolling happiness, oh what a sight,
Snack delight brings pure delight!

Saucy drizzles, a flavor parade,
In every bite, smiles are made.
Lettuce whispers, spice is bold,
This pocket of joy never gets old.

Crunchy corners, oh what fun,
Bites that make you rise and run.
Giggles burst with every chew,
Who knew food could giggle too?

Napkin ready for any spill,
Joyful feast is never still.
Delightful bites and laughter blend,
A tasty hug, my hungry friend!

Swaddled Sensations

Cozy wraps, snug as a hug,
Flavors dance like a playful bug.
Every layer hides a jest,
In savory folds, we find the best.

Salsa splashes, laughter flows,
In this cuddle, everyone knows.
Cheesy treasures tightly swathed,
Here's a meal that's gently bathed.

Roll it tight, don't let it fall,
Cravings rise, we heed the call.
Warm and fuzzy, smiles abound,
In every roll, good vibes are found.

A spoon, a fork? Oh, what a bore!
Let's dive in, who needs the chore?
Wrapped in joy, munch and play,
Food and laughter are here to stay!

Tasteful Tucks

Tucked away in wraps so bright,
Goodness layered, pure delight.
Each scrumptious layer, a surprise,
Joy unfolds, oh how it flies!

Shimmery beans and rice unite,
Spicy twists, oh what a sight!
Mirthful munching, feelings soar,
In every bite we laugh for more.

Craving hugs in every fold,
Comfort served in flavors bold.
These little rolls bring out my cheer,
With each bite, my worries disappear.

So gather round, let's have a feast,
Where giggles rise and troubles cease.
Wrapped in warmth, what a delight,
In soulful bites, we take flight!

Fleecy Feasts

With a cozy wrap around my hand,
A feast so warm, oh isn't it grand?
Colors dance in every fold,
Flavors mixed, a story told.

Mop the plate with happy grins,
Laugh as the tasty adventure begins.
Stuffed with dreams and savory flair,
In every nook, joy's everywhere!

Roll it up, let's not be shy,
Here's a hug that's hard to deny.
Every crunch brings a joyful sound,
In this feast, pure fun is found.

Chasing flavors all around,
With each bite, silliness abound.
Let's celebrate this tasty spree,
In a cozy wrap, it's you and me!

Cozy Cuisine

Warm wrap on my lap, it's snuggling time,
Filled with beans and dreams, oh that's sublime!
Salsa giggles and cheese in a hug,
The plate is a party, just give it a tug.

Chips in the air, they want to join in,
A crunchy eruption, wearing a grin.
Avocado whispers, 'Come dip with me',
While sour cream rolls, 'Let's dance with glee!'

Each bite's a soft laugh, full of delight,
In the kitchen's warm glow, everything's bright.
Tortilla giggles, 'I'm snug like a bug',
While spices shimmy, just giving a hug.

So here, in this bliss, we all come around,
A feast of good times, joy can be found.
Wrapped in these flavors, together we play,
In this cozy cuisine, we'll laugh all day.

Clad in Flavor

Dressed in layers, a flavor parade,
Each bite a costume, in the grand charade.
Lettuce twirls as it leaps on the scene,
While tomato juggles, quite the cuisine!

Rice does the tango, a grainy delight,
Beans join the party, a wholesome sight.
Peppers paint smiles with bursts of bright hue,
In this grand banquet, everyone's new.

Sippin' on zing and salsa surprise,
The taste buds giggle, oh how they rise!
Here's to the spices that dance on our tongues,
In this jazzy feast, no one's ever young.

So roll up your fun, wrap tight like a cheer,
With laughter and flavor, let's all persevere.
In this clad of flavor, we're snug as can be,
So share in the joy, let yourself be free!

Tantalizing Textiles

Soft and smooth, like a warm embrace,
Here lies a cushion, a savory space.
Wrapped in delights, with herbs fresh and wild,
In this culinary quilt, I'm a happy child.

Toppings are friends, they're giggling with cheer,
Together they mingle, spreading warmth here.
Sauces are streamers, bright colors they bring,
In this edible fabric, let's all start to sing.

Textures collide, a playful dance,
With every mouthful, let's take a chance.
It's a fiesta of flavors, a party of taste,
In these tantalizing textiles, don't let it go to waste.

So wrap up the joy, in layers of fun,
With humor and flavor, let's all come undone.
In this fiesta of snacks, laughter's the key,
Tantalizing textiles, together we're free!

Softly Seasoned

Gentle whispers of garlic and spice,
Each bite a giggle, oh so nice!
Warmth like a blanket, snug and tight,
In every delicious mouthful, pure delight.

Salsa's a poet, telling sweet tales,
Cilantro adds color, like vibrant sails.
A sprinkle of laughter, a dash of cheer,
Softly seasoned flavors, keep bringing us near.

With every wrap, we join in the fun,
Each savory journey has just begun.
In this hug of food, we all intertwine,
With creamy surprises, let's toast with fine wine.

So gather around, for a feast that feels right,
With soft, seasoned joys that lift us in flight.
In this festive kitchen, where laughter is spun,
Let's savor these moments, 'till the day is done.

Feast of Fabric and Fillings

In a world of fluff and crunch,
Where flavors mingle, take a lunch,
A tortilla hug, so warm and nice,
A picnic treat, oh, how to entice!

With salsa drip and cheese that melts,
Spices dance, oh, how it helps,
Wrapped up snug, like a cozy dream,
Eating bliss, a joyful theme!

Giggling bites, a tasty mess,
Sauce on hands, I must confess,
Laughter rolls like doughy wraps,
In this feast, we share our chaps!

So let us munch with silly glee,
In comfort's arms, we're fancy-free,
A banquet bright, with fun displays,
In fabric folds, we spend our days!

Dreams Rolled Tight

In a tortilla land, I wander wide,
With fillings tucked, and taste to ride,
Beans and cheese, they play so bold,
Each round bite, a joy retold.

A roll of fun, with guac on top,
I giggle loud, I eat non-stop,
Each savory hug wraps dreams so bright,
A silly feast, a pure delight!

With every munch, the world feels right,
Dancing flavors, what a sight,
Wrapped in joy, we laugh and cheer,
In this warm wrap, there's no fear!

So take a bite, let laughter flow,
In tasty hugs, our spirits grow,
Dreams rolled tight, we'll share a bite,
A smorgasbord of pure delight!

Softness Meets Savory

A fluffy blanket with savory flair,
Two comforts meet, oh what a pair,
Spicy blends and textures soft,
In cozy wraps, our spirits loft.

With every fold, a giggle spills,
Flavors dance like jubilant thrills,
Wrap me up, in laughter's cheer,
Each tasty mouthful brings us near.

A drizzle here, a sprinkle there,
Sauce on faces, oh, what a scare,
In delicious hugs, we find our bliss,
A crispy crunch, we can't resist!

So gather round, for joy's embrace,
In soft surrounds, we share our grace,
Beneath the wrap, let laughter play,
Savory softness leads the way!

The Comfort of Heated Wraps

When the chill bites, we close the gap,
With snug delights, we take a nap,
Warmth and crunch, a lovely sight,
In cozy folds, our laughs ignite.

Heated hugs, a joyful round,
In every layer, love is found,
As flavors pop, our spirits soar,
A warm embrace, who could want more?

With sizzle, drizzle, joy on plates,
Let's gather 'round, celebrate fates,
Each tasty treat, a cheerful thrill,
In bites of joy, our hearts are still.

So share a wrap, let giggles thrive,
In laughter's arms, we feel alive,
Warm and cozy, what a cap,
In the comfort of our heated wrap!

Delightful Duvets

Wrapped snug in a cozy hug,
A feast in each fold, oh what a drug.
Salsa spills, a colorful sight,
Under covers, we laugh through the night.

Laughter erupts as crumbs dance,
In soft warmth, we take a chance.
A fiesta hidden, oh what a treat,
With every bite, our hearts skip a beat.

Snoozing through flavors, the perfect plan,
Chasing tacos, like a playful span.
Late-night munchies, dreams intertwine,
In this soft realm, everything's divine.

The world outside fades, we're tucked away,
In our culinary bubble, come what may.
Who knew joy came wrapped so tight,
In this silly blend, we find pure delight.

Textures of Taste

In fluffy layers, we dream and eat,
A zesty mix is quite the feat.
Wrapped in fun, we dive right in,
With every bite, laughter begins.

Oh, the squish of savory tricks,
In this cocoon, we find our fix.
A dash of spice, a tickle of zest,
Comfy goodness, we simply jest.

Between bites, we share a grin,
As we dive into the cozy din.
Each flavor swirl, a playful dance,
In warm arms, we take a chance.

So grab a napkin, take a seat,
Where warmth and crunch are quite the treat.
In this adventure of taste, we play,
With giggles wrapped in a savory ballet.

Silken Savor

A blanket of comfort, a tasty embrace,
Each nibble brings joy, no time to waste.
Delicious dreams in layers unfold,
Soft warmth wraps us, magical and bold.

Oh, the flavors that twirl and spin,
In twinkling delight, where do we begin?
Smiles and leftovers, a happy mix,
Under the warmth, it's pure food tricks.

Giggles rise as sauce takes flight,
Dance of the crunchy, a merry delight.
Each hidden bite holds a spicy surprise,
In this cozy space, pure joy multiplies.

So let's toast to leftovers and cozy dreams,
Where each meal bursts with laughter, or so it seems.
With nose to the feast, together we sway,
In silken layers, we always find play.

Flavor-Filled Shawls

In a snug cocoon of warmth we roll,
A bounty of goodies that makes us whole.
Each flavor wrapped in a soft embrace,
We giggle and munch at our own pace.

Crumbs tumble down as laughter rings,
In our plush haven, joy freely flings.
Salsa sun rays warm the cozy space,
As we recount tales with smiles on our face.

A buffet of bites, a friendship bound,
In the blanket realm, there's magic found.
Mouthfuls of joy mixed with a dash,
Under this dome, we share a laugh.

So let's celebrate with this funny feast,
Where happiness grows and worries cease.
In each layer, a new fond tale,
Flavor-filled warmth that will always prevail.

Snuggly Slices

In a tortilla wrap so tight,
Laughter rolls like a cozy kite.
Cheesy dreams take flight on high,
Wrapped in comfort, we'll all comply.

Beans and salsa join the dance,
With a twirl, they take their chance.
Under layers, joy is spun,
A playful feast, oh what fun!

Flavors mingle, making glee,
Like a hug from a warm cup of tea.
Wiggling bites with every chomp,
As we giggle, we can't stop!

A crunchy shell and soft embrace,
Savoring life at a speedy pace.
Napkins ready for the spill,
Happiness wrapped up with skill.

Warming Wonders

Fluffy layers piled up tall,
Wrapped in joy, we'll have a ball.
Each savory mix, a delight,
Cuddled up, we munch all night.

Heat and spice make taste buds cheer,
Grinning wide from ear to ear.
Twirled around like a circus trick,
Each bite's a joyful little kick.

Spoonfuls of smiles in every fold,
A story of warmth, delicious and bold.
We laugh and share around the warm,
In this snuggly feast, we find our charm.

Salty and sweet, a perfect match,
With a little mess, oh what a catch!
Rolling in flavors, we can't resist,
Moments of joy we can't dismiss.

Nurtured Nourishment

A cozy wrap with a secret bite,
Each morsel brings pure delight.
Rolling laughter in every taste,
No time to waste, don't let it haste!

Saucy drizzles travel around,
In our nests, comfort is found.
Holding memories, warm and bright,
Savoring joy, from day to night.

Each tasty twist, a hug of zest,
In a playful dance, we're truly blessed.
Gathered close, we feast with cheer,
In delicious moments, we disappear.

Snacks unite, as giggles sound,
Wrapped in flavor, we're glory-bound.
Bites of happiness we adore,
In our hearts, we'll always want more.

Cradled Comforts

Delightful rolls of scrumptious fare,
Lick the fingers, flavors to share.
Sitting snug, outside the chill,
With every crunch, we find our thrill.

Smoky bliss, a spirited vibe,
Peak of laughter as we tribe.
With salsa steps and cheesy sway,
In this wrap, we'll laugh and play.

A merry mix in a tasty shell,
Bouncing flavors, they ring a bell.
Under layers, stories unfold,
In this embrace, we feel such gold.

Each nibble tickles silly bone,
This quirky spread, we call our own.
Fun and warmth in every bite,
In a canvas of joy, everything's right!

Whirl of Flavor

A dance of wraps and cheesy dreams,
With laughter spilling at the seams.
Veggies tumble, salsa splashes,
It's a fiesta in delicious flashes.

Guacamole winks, a playful tease,
Spicy bites bring you to your knees.
Tortillas twirl like a dancer's feet,
Each mouthful a party, oh so sweet!

With every crunch, a giggle breaks,
Filling up, oh what a stakes!
In a cozy spot, we twine and cling,
As savory joys make our hearts sing.

So grab a fork, or just your hands,
In this whirlwind, joy expands.
As we unwrap each tasty treat,
Life's too short—let laughter repeat!

Hearth and Harmony

Gather 'round, let's share a cheer,
With rolls of warmth, we've nothing to fear.
Flavorful hugs wrapped snug and tight,
Filling up our hearts each night.

A sprinkle of spice, a dollop of cheer,
Each bite a memory, fond and dear.
As friends all gather, stories unfurl,
In this tranquil nook, flavors whirl.

Sizzle and crunch create the sound,
Laughter and joy where love is found.
Every bite an embrace, so divine,
In this savory world, we all intertwine.

Comfort is served, just take a seat,
Where hearty delights and friendships meet.
In spicy warmth, our spirits align,
Together we savor, and all is fine.

Savory Swaddles

Wrapped snugly in layers of glee,
Spice and laughter, oh, come share with me.
Each fold a secret, each bite a thrill,
In cozy corners, our hearts we fill.

Herbs and cheese join the playful fray,
While salsa's splash makes dullness sway.
Comfort food with a twist of zest,
A humorous journey on a tasty quest.

In the warmth of this delightful scene,
With quirky flavors, our joy's unseen.
Beneath the stars, with smiles and cheer,
Each wrapped creation wipes away fear.

So let's embark on this culinary ride,
In every fold, let laughter reside.
We'll roll into dreams on this comfy bed,
With flavors and gags dancing in our head.

Warm Embrace of Delight

Oh, the joy of a tasty embrace,
Saucy smiles, a spicy face.
With laughter bubbling like a hot stew,
Each mouthful more than just a scoop or two.

The table's set, it's a colorful spread,
Wrapped treasures dancing in the bread.
Giggles erupt with every bite,
As flavors collide in pure delight.

With each soft wrap, a cuddle so fine,
A playful mix, all in a line.
Savor the moments, let's not be shy,
In this funny feast, let spirits fly.

So come together, my hungry friends,
In this cozy fiesta, laughter lends.
With every sandwich, a hug we shout,
In delicious delight, we'll never tap out!

Enveloping Euphoria

In a tortilla's hug, I find my peace,
Salsa and cheese bring me sweet release.
Roll me up tight, don't let me go,
I'll be your burrito, put on a show.

With each tasty bite, my worries fade,
Guacamole dreams, a flavor parade.
Chips on the side, crunching so sweet,
This wrap of joy can't be beat!

A blanket of flavor, cozy and warm,
In this culinary storm, I'm safe from harm.
Dance with me, flavors so bright,
Together we'll laugh into the night.

So grab a hot sauce, let's take a trip,
Life's too short for a boring dip.
In this wrap of fun, we'll roll along,
With every bite, we'll hum our song.

Wrapped Delights

A cozy creation, a feast for the eyes,
Wrapped up so snug, it's a tasty surprise.
Stuffed to the brim with all that's divine,
Each savory layer, a treasure to find.

Potato, beans, and a sprinkle of zest,
Over-the-top joy in this flavor fest.
Lettuce and meat in a happy embrace,
One big bite puts a grin on my face.

So pass me the salsa, let's make it rain,
Dancing flavors, a wild champagne.
In each little wrap, oh what a ride,
A carnival taste that I cannot hide.

Cheese melting slowly, like dreams in a dance,
Join me in bliss, oh take a chance!
With every crunchy chip, we'll soar and dive,
In this tasty wrap, we truly thrive!

Cradled in Culinary Joy

Cradled within a tortilla's warmth,
Filling me up like a late-night charm.
Each bite like laughter, I can't get enough,
In this edible hug, life's so tough!

From spices that tingle to sauces that splash,
Flavors collide in a glorious clash.
It's a festival of fun on every plate,
Wrapped up in joy, oh, isn't it great?

Tangled in toppings, let's lose all the stress,
A culinary hug, I must confess.
With layers of love, we take a big dive,
In this pocket of bliss, we truly thrive.

So here's to the creations that make us all cheer,
Full of delight, bringing good times near.
With each savory treasure, we giggle and munch,
In this world of wraps, let's have a big lunch!

Warm Nurture

Snug as a bug, wrapped so tight,
Delicious surprises make it all right.
Sour cream swirls in a dance of delight,
With every warm blanket, the flavors ignite.

Diced veggies tumble in a playful swirl,
As the sauces mix, my heart starts to twirl.
It's not just a meal, it's a cozy embrace,
Bringing smiles and laughter, a happy place.

With a crunch for the ages and bites full of zest,
In this joyful wrap, we're feeling our best.
So wear your napkin, it's messy but fun,
In this fiesta feast, we've only begun.

Let's giggle and munch till the day turns to night,
In each tasty morsel, the world feels just right.
In this warmth we share, let's savor the ride,
With smiles and flavors all wrapped up inside.

Veiled Vigor

Wrapped up tight with zest on fire,
Every bite ignites a wild desire.
Beans and cheese in a cozy fold,
A culinary hug that never gets old.

Laughter rolls as flavors blend,
Tortilla tales that never end.
Chasing crumbs like a puppy's play,
In this tasty land, we laugh and stay.

Salsa tangs like jokes gone wild,
A fiesta feast for the inner child.
With every munch, a giggle escapes,
In a swirl of spice, joy takes shapes.

So come unwind, let's have some fun,
Under the stars, our feast begun.
With every roll, the night is bright,
Jubilant munching 'til morning light.

Soft Layers of Flavor

A plush embrace of taste awaits,
In velvety folds, we celebrate.
Chili whispers and guacamole dreams,
In this plush world, a giggle screams.

Layers of joy, wrapped snug and neat,
Filling hearts with warm, savory treat.
Tucked in tight, with a smile so wide,
In this cozy feast, jokes sneaking inside.

Beans and rice, a merry affair,
With a crunchy sidekick, we don't care.
As laughter sparkles and flavors dance,
Every tasty bite becomes a new chance.

So grab a fork, let the fun unfold,
In our soft haven, be brave, be bold.
With silly sides and a hearty delight,
We'll munch our way to the moon tonight.

Culinary Cocooning

Snuggled up in a tortilla dream,
Where flavors swirl and giggles beam.
Adding layers, like a silly game,
In this food cocoon, no two bites the same.

Toppings tumble, a hilarious mess,
Sour cream clouds, dressed to impress.
With every crunch, a chuckle might leak,
In this feast of fun, no need to be meek.

Here comes the salsa, with a cheeky grin,
Diving in headfirst, oh where to begin?
A wrap so snug, it hugs back tight,
In this culinary hug, everything feels right.

So cozy up, let the munchies roll,
As we laugh and bite, we'll share the whole bowl.
In this riotous romp, all taste buds sing,
Wrapped in joy, it's a wonderful thing.

Tempting Tufts

Come gather 'round for a crunchy tale,
As flavors mingle, laughter sets sail.
Wrapped in warmth, these treasures surprise,
Filling our bellies and brightening eyes.

Puffy pillows with a spicy twist,
In this savory chaos, who can resist?
Every nibble's a joke, every bite's a cheer,
In this whimsical world, there's nothing to fear.

From shredded goodness to melted bliss,
Each soft layer a giggle, can you guess?
With flavors dancing like a silly waltz,
In these tasty moments, we forget all faults.

So let's indulge in this feasting spree,
With every taste, we just can't flee.
For in this cozy, tasty retreat,
Life's a fiesta, oh so sweet!

Layers of Love and Texture

In a wrap so snug and round,
Flavors dance, joy is found.
Cheese and beans, a playful tease,
Each layer stacks, with such ease.

A spicy sip, a crunchy bite,
This crafty feast feels just right.
With each fold, a secret held,
In soft corners, joy is swelled.

The salsa smiles, the guac's a tease,
Together wrapped, we laugh with ease.
In every bite, a giggle sparks,
A savory ride, with tasty marks.

So gather 'round, let's share a laugh,
This simple meal, our happy path.
Each layer wraps a tale so bright,
In cozy fun, we share the night.

Savory Shelters

Under wraps, we find our glee,
A tasty hideaway for you and me.
With zesty notes in cozy folds,
This cuddly feast, a treasure holds.

Wrapped in warmth, no chill in sight,
We dive in deep, with pure delight.
Lettuce crisp and sauces bold,
In every bite, our laughter unfolds.

A chili kick, a cooling dollop,
Each mouthful begs for a joyful follow-up.
In this snug wrap, our spirits soar,
With every crunch, we laugh for more.

So let's indulge in this embrace,
A snack so fun, it wins the race.
In our scrumptious lair, we'll stay,
With flavors bright, come what may.

Tasteful Warmth

When comfort calls in tasty ways,
We cozy up, through laughter's rays.
A soft embrace, with bold delight,
Warmth unrolls, with every bite.

Filled with goodies, wrapped so neat,
This handheld smile, can't be beat.
Zesty bursts and creamy swirls,
Each bite a mix of culinary pearls.

A pinch of spice, a mellow flare,
In each fold lies love and care.
We gather close, with plates in hand,
Wrapped in joy, a merry band.

So let us feast, let worries fade,
In our warm nest, we've got it made.
With every layer snugly placed,
We celebrate in tasty haste.

A Soft Symphony of Ingredients

In a tender wrap, flavors play,
A giggle fest, come what may.
Each ingredient sings a tune,
Dancing together, morning to noon.

Crispy edges, lush inside,
A soft embrace, flavors collide.
With every roll, laughter flows,
A merry melody, as joy grows.

The garlic hums, the beans beat time,
In this happy wrap, we find our rhyme.
Together we chomp, in comical spree,
Crafting memories, just you and me.

So grab a friend, unroll a feast,
In every bite, life feels increased.
A soft symphony, flavors unite,
In this flavorful joy, we take flight.

Flavorful Blanketing

In a cozy wrap, I take a bite,
Spices dance, oh what a delight!
Salsa splatters, giggles arise,
Wrapped in laughter, beneath the skies.

Tortilla tales, filled to the brim,
With each new flavor, my heart starts to swim,
A pinch of humor, a twist of fate,
In this tasty hug, I can't be late.

Saucy secrets tucked inside,
Every munch is a thrilling ride,
When the chips fall, I seek a snack,
With cheesy grins, there's no turning back.

So let's roll up, let's have some fun,
With layers aplenty, I know I've won,
In this flavorful wrap, joy is complete,
A feast of smiles, can't be beat!

Hearth-cooked Hugs

Warmth from the oven, a scrumptious scene,
Filling my belly, that's the routine,
Savory chunks tucked in tight,
Every bite, pure delight!

Even cold days can't bring me down,
With cozy layers, I wear the crown,
Each gooey morsel, a laughter-filled hug,
Sticky fingers, that's how I snug.

With a side of beans, my joy increases,
As spicy giggles become my pieces,
In a warm embrace, I find my glee,
Comfort wrapped, just like me!

So come join the feast, let's share a grin,
With flavors and fun, where do we begin?
These hearth-cooked treasures are never a drag,
Just serve me love, in a tote or a bag!

Casuistic Coverings

What's rolled within? Oh, what a tease,
Mysteries wrapped like a playful breeze,
Laughter and layers, secrets untold,
In every bite, the joy unfolds.

Crunchy or soft? I can't decide,
With each little nibble, my heart skips wide,
Bubble-wrap bites, with a dash of spice,
This puzzle of flavors, oh, so nice!

Tangled tastes play tag in my mouth,
From north to south, they dance about,
With a wink and a laugh, I twist and turn,
In a flurry of flavors, my belly will churn.

So roll me up, let's dive right in,
In these quirky wraps, I know I'll win,
Combine the silly, the sweet, the bold,
In this crunchy hug, let fun unfold!

Cushioned Cravings

When hunger strikes, what do I find?
A treasure tucked, one of a kind,
Softened edges and zesty flair,
With every bite, I toss out despair.

A pillow of flavor in my warm hand,
I take a big bite, oh, isn't it grand?
Saucy goodness drips, oh what a mess,
With giggles and grins, I must confess.

Layers stacked high, such a cozy feel,
Each unwinding wrap, a comforting meal,
With friends all around, we munch and laugh,
In our cushioned joy, we find the path.

So gather round, let the filling flow,
In warmth and laughter, let happiness grow,
With flavors that dance and smiles that gleam,
In this snug feast, we all find our dream!

Flavors of Home

In a tortilla fold, oh the secrets they keep,
Beans and cheese dance, making taste buds leap.
Spices play hide and seek, a joyful parade,
Each bite a fiesta, all worries must fade.

Salsa is giggling, hot in the mix,
It quips and it quakes like a bag full of tricks.
Guacamole's grand, with its creamy delight,
A party on a plate, oh what a sight!

Wrapped snug and cozy, like a hug from the chef,
Every layer whispers, "You've got to feel blessed."
A mashup of flavors, a joyful reprise,
This meal's like a treasure, the ultimate prize.

So here's to our eatery, a place filled with cheer,
Where tastes collide madly and laughter's sincere.
Each mouthful a giggle, each crumb is a jest,
In this vibrant haven, we're forever a guest.

Soft Touch of Savor

Snuggled in softness, a joy to behold,
Each layer wrapped tightly, like stories untold.
Chili and laughter, they mingle so free,
A fluffy embrace, it's a feast for me.

Every bite bursts forth with a slapstick surprise,
Taco dreams mingling, oh how they rise!
Sour cream kisses, like shy little pals,
Play jump rope with jalapeños and pals.

This roll of pure joy, oh why do we wait?
Unraveling humor, it's never too late.
Crunchy and soft, like a giggle in motion,
Creating new flavors, a wacky devotion.

We'll share and enjoy, let the shenanigans flow,
With friends and good food, our smiles surely grow.
Wrapped up in a chuckle, a treat to devour,
Together we savor, oh what a power.

Enveloping Essence

In foils of delight, where treasures abound,
Mixtures of magic, where laughter is found.
Layers of joy in a colorful swirl,
Each taste is a giggle, in every twirl.

A blanket of flavors, all cozy and warm,
This meal is a hug, a savory charm.
Crispy shell crunch, like a giggling sound,
Our hearts are now dancing, joyfully unbound.

With coleslaw confetti, they sprinkle and toss,
A party on a platter, oh, what's the loss?
Spicy remarks, with a tangent or two,
Wrapped in a riddle, this feast speaks to you!

So here we convene, with a playful jest,
Eager to munch on this whimsical fest.
Each fold a reflection of fun we adore,
In this world of flavors, let's always explore.

Wrapped in Whimsy

In a swirl of the silly, we'll gather around,
A buffet of giggles, where smiles abound.
Each swirl of finesse brings a chuckle so sweet,
Tasting the essence, what a delightful treat!

Crunchy on one side, with wonders galore,
Splashing with joy, we can't help but explore.
Dressings of humor drizzled with cheer,
Wrapped in the flavors that bring us near.

The drama of dinners, a culinary show,
Savory plots thicken, and laughter will flow.
We toss and we share, in this joyous affair,
With bites of nostalgia and smiles in the air.

So lift up your forks, let's embrace the delight,
With quirky creations that dance through the night.
In whimsical harmony, together we feast,
With flavors and laughter, we're sharing the least.

Wrapped in Flavorful Caresses

A tortilla hug, oh what a sight,
Filled with joy, steaming and bright.
Around my waist, it snugly clings,
A savory dance, oh the joy it brings!

Cheddar and beans, a cheesy delight,
Rolling my eyes with every bite.
Like a warm friend on a chilly day,
In this tasty wrap, I'll forever stay!

Peppers, onions, all snug and tight,
Making my tummy feel just right.
Every layer, a giggle and grin,
Who knew comfort could wrap me in?

So pass the salsa and let's enjoy,
This happiness served, oh boy, oh boy!
In every fold, a cheerful cheer,
Life's silly moments brought so near!

Cozy Packages

Packages of joy, all snug and round,
In their warm holds, contentment is found.
Wrapped in layers of tasty embrace,
A little bite of a happy place.

With every crunch, my heart takes flight,
A delightful wrapper in soft sunlight.
Like cuddly pets on a lazy day,
These cozy creations lead me astray!

Filling spills out, oh what a mess,
But with each giggle, I love it no less.
Gather 'round, it's a feast we'll share,
In this hilarious food-filled affair!

So let's roll up and take a big bite,
Wrapped up snug, what pure delight!
Laughter and warmth at every turn,
In my comfy treat, my heart will yearn!

The Art of Comfort Hospitality

Hospitality wrapped up so nice,
Stuffed with flavors that entice.
A symphony of crunch and goo,
Who needs a chair when I've got you?

Each bite's a hug from all around,
A spicy welcome that knows no bound.
Friends gather close, laughter in the air,
Shared rolls of comfort, beyond compare!

Layer upon layer of joy and cheer,
In this warm meal, our troubles clear.
Pico de gallo, a splash of zest,
Bringing us closer, it's simply the best!

So join the feast, don't be shy,
In our delicious realms, let's soar and fly!
The art of comfort, we hold so dear,
In every savory bite, love draws near!

Tender Rolls and Tightly Woven Tales

Tender rolls with stories to tell,
Each tasty layer, a flavor spell.
Wrapped around laughter and playful chats,
Who knew comfort could come like that?

Happiness spilled in every fold,
A warm surprise, bright and bold.
With a tiny crunch and a cheeky smile,
These vivid delights are worth the while!

Dip in the sauce, let chaos reign,
Twirling and swirling, it's hard to contain.
Every bite we take sparks a tale,
In this funny feast, we will never fail!

So gather your friends, it's time for some fun,
These woven rolls are number one!
In the tales of laughter, joy prevails,
Tender moments in our tightly woven tales.

A Warm Roll of Delight

A tortilla wrap of joy, so tight,
Filled with beans, a savory bite.
Chasing crumbs with a napkin's might,
This tasty treat brings pure delight.

Salsa drips like a belly laugh,
Guacamole's a creamy path.
Each bite's a giggle, a fun photograph,
In the world of snacks, it reigns by math.

Lettuce crunches, a playful sound,
With every roll, joy's truly found.
Spicy adventures that know no bound,
In this wrap of happiness, we're all crowned.

So gather 'round for a feast of glee,
Serve it up with a side of free.
Wipe those hands, shout with glee,
In every roll, life's jubilee.

Hidden Treasures in Fabric

Under layers soft and warm, we nest,
Snug and tight, where dreams can rest.
Whispers of comfort, a cozy jest,
In folds of warmth, we feel the best.

Within the folds, delights await,
A little snack shared on our plate.
Hidden treasures await our fate,
In this fabric fortress, we celebrate.

Crinkling wrappers, oh what a sound,
As we munch with laughter all around.
Each bite a giggle, flavors abound,
In our cozy haven, joy is found.

So cuddle up with a snack or two,
In this plush embrace, we'll laugh right through.
With bites and chuckles, a merry crew,
In our soft cocoon, the world feels new.

Comfort Food Cradled

Wrapped tight like a warm embrace,
Savory goodness, a great escape.
In a world of chaos, this delightful place,
With every chew, we find our grace.

Melting cheese, oh what a dream,
A laughter-filled snack, a perfect scheme.
With each crispy edge, we hear the theme,
Joy is simple, or so it seems.

In soft folds, we feel the bliss,
Playful bites that we can't resist.
A hearty chuckle, sealed with a kiss,
In this cradled comfort, life's pure mist.

So gather your friends, let's make a night,
With tasty treasures and laughter's light.
Share these delights, hold each other tight,
In food and fun, everything's right.

Snug Bites and Soft Nights

With cuddly layers, we dive right in,
Crunchy bites that make the grin.
In a soft cocoon where giggles begin,
Late-night munchies, let's begin the win.

Rolled up goodness, a feast to share,
Spilling flavors without a care.
A sprinkle of laughter to fill the air,
In this cozy corner, we bond and dare.

A brew of friendship in every wrap,
As we gather 'round, a playful map.
Filling our hearts, no need for a gap,
In bites of joy, we all take a nap.

So let's enjoy our snug delights,
With blankets of laughter on quirky nights.
Together we conquer, facing our sights,
In this world of wraps, everything ignites.

Snuggle into Savory

In a cozy nook, I start to munch,
Wrapped delights make quite the brunch.
Bean and cheese, dance on my tongue,
Saucy surprises make me feel young.

Chasing crumbs with giggles and sighs,
Laughter erupts, oh how she flies!
Salsa splatters, a colorful mess,
Who knew snacks could cause such excess?

Tortilla hug, a flavorful shell,
Each bite whispers, 'Oh, taste this well!'
Velvet texture, a cuddle so nice,
A spicy swirl adds extra spice.

With every chomp, the world seems bright,
Snuggled up tight, everything feels right.
Join the feast, let the good times roll,
In this tasty world, we all play a role.

Serene Wraps of Flavor

Nestled in layers, a savory dream,
Every mouthful makes me want to scream.
Lettuce peeks out, crisp and so green,
A hug of taste, you'd know what I mean.

Spices tango upon my eager lips,
Each savory wrap, oh what fun trips!
Saucy wonders join the tasty fray,
Each adventure starts with a bold parfait.

Morsels that dance and wiggle with glee,
Cuddled in warmth, just my snack and me.
The joy of a bite, a delicious embrace,
Flavor-filled magic, a savory space.

Crunching and munching till all is gone,
Laughing out loud, from dusk until dawn.
In a tangle of joy, I'll take my seat,
For cozy wraps, they just can't be beat!

Wrapped Warmth

Huddled close, a snacking delight,
Warmth envelops, everything feels right.
Cheese drips slow, a gooey delight,
Oh, these tasty treasures, wrap me up tight!

Giggles bubble as sauces splash,
An epic fight with guac, oh what a clash!
I roll and I tumble, flavors collide,
In this delicious game, we'll take each stride.

Crunchy edges, soft and sublime,
In this silly dance, we savor the time.
Melon laughter and spicy charms,
Their cozy embrace brings joy in swarms.

So here we feast, in warmth and cheer,
In every bite, there's no room for fear.
Let's wrap it up, let's take our fill,
With coziness here, we'll munch at will.

Cozy Creations

Oh what a mess, what a scrumptious sight,
With flavors colliding, it's pure delight.
Dressed in toppings, the colors so bright,
We dive into laughter, a culinary flight.

Each bite's an adventure, a silly surprise,
Where dreams of snacks dance before our eyes.
A rolled-up joy that's hearty and fun,
In this tasty escapade, we've only begun.

Melted goodness and hearty beans meet,
Plated with humor, the perfect treat.
Sharing the laughter, we munch down with grace,
In this cozy moment, we've found our place.

So join me now, let's savor and play,
In this tasty journey, we'll find our way.
With chuckles and crumbs, let the good times flow,
Wrapped in this joy, our hearts will glow!

Flavors Under Covers

Wrapped in warmth, a feast awaits,
A cozy roll where laughter mates.
Seasoned dreams in every bite,
A dance of spice that feels just right.

Salsa giggles, guac's a tease,
Stuffing joy, it's sure to please.
Peppers whisper, beans compose,
Each mouthful hidden, joy overflows.

Under layers soft and grand,
Filling fun in every strand.
Unraveled cheer, a savory joke,
With every chew, a smile woke.

When hunger calls, don't fret or fear,
Flavors bundled, drawing near.
In this wrap of tasty cheer,
We find delight, our hearts adhere.

Tasteful Tufts

A fluffy feast of flavors bold,
Wrapped so snug, they never get cold.
Each bite a giggle, a savory laugh,
In this fluffy world, we dance and chaff.

Crispy edges, soft embrace,
Dancing spices in a joyous race.
Dip and dive, a crunch parade,
In blankets of joy, we're unafraid.

Saucy winks and cheesy grins,
Life's too short for duller spins.
With each soft layer, stories unfold,
Delicious secrets in folds of gold.

Toasty shells and filling dreams,
Feasting together, bursting seams.
Wrapped up tight, we share the glee,
In a world of flavor, just you and me.

Edible Hugs

A hug that's tasty, warm, and round,
In every fold, good vibes are found.
Savoring wraps that squeeze with glee,
Feeling the warmth, just you and me.

Roasted corn and zesty flair,
Stuffed with joy beyond compare.
Squeeze it tight, don't let it go,
Hugs of flavor steal the show.

Snuggled bites that make us grin,
Laughter's seasoning to let us win.
Each savory crunch, a playful tease,
Tender moments wrapped with ease.

In these cozy, tasty swirls,
We find connection, joy unfurls.
So take a bite, embrace the fun,
In every hug, the flavor's spun.

Plush Pleasures

Soft delights in every fold,
Wrapped in warmth, a story told.
Filling flavors, sassy and bright,
A feast of laughter, pure delight.

Cheesy grins and crunchy hugs,
Each layer packed with edible bugs.
But fear not, they're tasty treats,
In this plush realm, joy repeats.

Creamy dreams and spicy bliss,
With each soft munch, a flavor kiss.
Cozy wraps, our hearts entwine,
In a world of flavor, we dine divine.

With foil cozied 'round our snacks,
We gather round, sharing cracks.
So let's roll up and eat away,
In plush pleasures, we laugh and play.

Cozy Culinary Wraps

In a warm tortilla hug, I find my glee,
Stuffed with beans, oh what a spree!
Salsa drips like joy in the sun,
Each bite a party, oh what fun!

Cheese melting like dreams on a cold day,
Crispy edges lead my taste buds astray.
Lettuce crinkles like laughter's sweet song,
Wrapped up snug, where I belong!

Avocado whispers secrets so smooth,
Making each munch a cozy groove.
With every layer, my worries flee,
This roll of happiness comforts me.

In every corner, there's flavor to spare,
I twirl my napkin like I just don't care.
A dance of delight in my hand, oh dear,
Join me, my friend, for a wrap and a cheer!

Cherished Cravings

When hunger strikes like a playful tease,
I dream of wraps that are sure to please.
Stuffed with treasures, oh what a treat,
A dance of flavors, oh so neat!

Tomatoes tumble like giggles so bright,
Each ingredient mingles, pure delight.
I chase my cravings with joyous glee,
My trusty wrap, you're dear to me!

With every bite, a burst of fun,
Ranch dressing pools, oh what a run!
The world can wait, I've found my bliss,
In this savory swirl, I cannot miss.

A side of chips, it's a happy affair,
With nacho cheese and a whole lot to share.
Giggles erupt with each cheesy dip,
In this feast of delight, let's take a trip!

Cradled in Flavor

A fluffy wrap holds all my dreams,
Packed with goodness, bursting at the seams.
Each mouthful is magic, what a delight,
In this culinary hug, everything feels right.

Sour cream clouds float oh so high,
As flavors tango and twirl, oh my!
I'll dip and dive in a salsa sea,
Every bite is a new mystery!

Crunchy bits sing with each gentle chew,
Wrapped tight in joy, nothing feels blue.
A sprinkle of spice, a dash of sweet,
Each glorious mouthful is a playful treat.

Like a cozy quilt on a rainy day,
These tasty rolls keep the blues at bay.
So here's to good times and meals that thrill,
In this wrapping world, we feast at will!

Whimsical Wraps

Under the moon, I crave a delight,
A goofy bundle with flavors so bright.
Wrapped up snug like a loving hug,
In a dance of taste, I give a shrug!

Veggies prance in the soft embrace,
Spicy and sweet, they quicken the pace.
With whipped toppings that swirl and twirl,
Each playful bite makes my heart whirl.

The lunchtime circus comes to my plate,
As I twirl a tortilla with glee, oh great!
Churros on the side, let's make it a dance,
In this kitchen carnival, I take a chance!

So stack those layers, let's get it on,
With silly flavors until they're all gone.
For life's too short to eat just plain,
Let's wrap up wonder, and feel no shame!